[abjections]
=evan reynolds

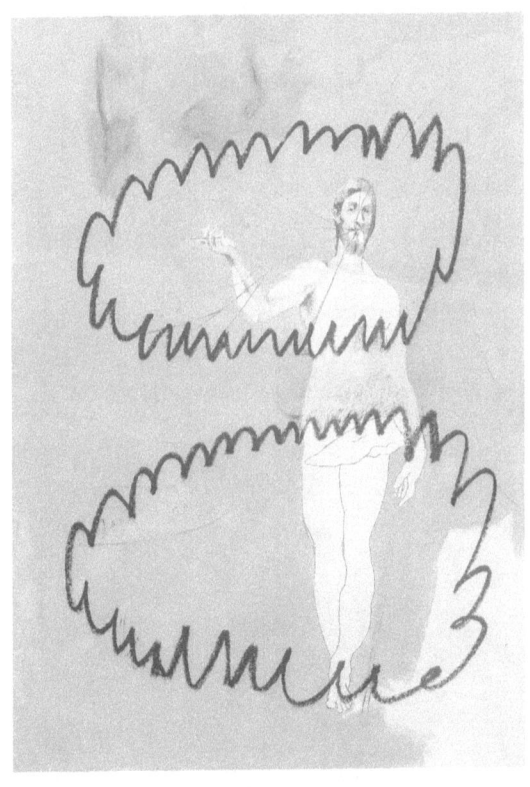

SPUYTEN DUYVIL
New York City

© 2024 Evan Reynolds

ISBN 978-1-959556-84-8

cover art by Matt Bodett

Library of Congress Control Number: 2023950774

[abjection]

subject refuses to sleep

subject insists that he has secret knowledge of a conspiracy involving the cia and large pharmaceutical companies

subject walks obsessively down the corridor in the same direction

subject refuses medication

subject does not wash or brush teeth

subject insists on talking to a lawyer

subject pulls at hair

subject stares out the window consistently

subject refuses therapy

subject rocks back and forth

subject displays writing behavior

subject continues to write

subject will not stop writing

subject will not stop writing

subject will not stop writing

subject will not stop writing

subject will not stop writing:

[ethereal]

"Music, rhythm, rigadoon, without end, for no reason."

—Julia Kristeva

[abjection]

my anemic breath sputtering

like a radiant shower of shit

he does not answer nor the

impact accreting in spindle-

like cosmic waves before me

across the chasm of encounter

i call to the other in the mirror

casting the violent shatter on

lines converging and diverging

on the canvas of my undoing

hostile winds cross-pollinate

through the expanding chasm

fragments which charge each

measured strike against whole

expanding feasts of shattering

the cross of gaps radiating

refracted against the parting

fissure to connect on every

enclosure which feeds the

ferocious fleeting encounter

[abjection]

i feel the light circle round about me like a talon to the soft tissue:

the pulsing radiant smear of skin on

bone projects the angle

at which

i

come undone

to the feral instinct digging

on my brain, beckoning me to release

and reconcile my impulses with the suppressive force of talons:

the hour projects on the surface of the screen like wild sunlight

cavernous waves giving way to

tearing apart the organs

everything under

will

come apart

at the feeble seams

the last desperate consonant scream

remains in fragmented unity with all the other jagged parts

[abjection]

ex nihilo abjure the post- claim silk

baggage engage supra terminal trauma

supposition command didactic chimera

sly fortification autumnal synchronic

doleful exegesis fou laurel condition

somnial cumulus triangulation cloven

autoimmune catachrestic sloth pulsation

[abjection]

fragments of my body scattered   across the floor   in no particular order
they seem to cluster

   in correlated trajectories   graph paper delusions   representational
organs

each piece of the fallout   a victim of separation   science creating the
world in its image

   my image is terse   refracted constellations   loose federations   of
subjects and objects

torn apart   and scattered around   in no particular order

[abjection]

the words emerge from deep within my thoughts, swing right and trace a path across the page, spiraling into themselves with feverish abandon, curling into their own path like a strange verbal snake coiling into a retainer of warmth against the chill of background noise inflecting these dimensions like declension of space looming up into the ether across this universe into the thing itself twisting, angled folding into all a swarm of words collapsing

[abjection]

angular momentum of verbal reckoning,
the lines slide in and out like lock pins
traversing the system rendered by each
deployment of syntax. a coded message
emerges from an exercise of morphology:
stillness of form clashes with motion of
function. a particularity undermines the
totality. when the schizo speaks, the room
falls dead silent with puzzlement. break-
in of disjunct babbling confuses grounds
from foreground: the world is a mess and
the mirror the schizo holds to the world
reveals its dimensions and composition.

[abjection]

the grammar of a fart sublimates

the rage of repression. when the

vicissitudes of homeostasis reign

terror on the possibility of becoming,

chimeric unfolding digs into

the virtual space of divine gas.

a map has no tenor and the vehicle

runs away with dissolving cognition.

[abjection]

sludge fills my mouth when i speak
like raw worms. i chew until
the insides of my mouth bleed.

the drugs compel a motion so hard
and muddled, the mouth loses its
ability to speak with any clarity.

tardive dyskinesia sounds just as
it is: the sharp teeth of consonants
against the garbled flesh of vowels.

[abjection]

after Jackson Mac Low

oedipal cigarette subtend amplification circumscription

tardive dyskinesia sublime manifold carotid circulate

implosion grammar damnation hallucinatory endive

fleering exclamation coniferous juxtaposition game

summit voodoo insect defecate completion insistence

refusal acceptance consecration ordained cosmological

profanation accelerate spiral autonomous

digestive peripheral courier thunders sacrament

concretion scale reverb exercise commissariat

echo ether contiguous centrifugal exegesis

neural context submission pasteurize scaffold

one hand clapping bronchial saussure plastic

confirmatory transient cyclone it collision erratic

sentimentality ersatz corrosive slither gaulish

focus conciliatory representation allusive coagulate

seminal ballistic subliminal break paragraph style

atmospheric slum suppletion corroborative fish

centripetal guesswork fire claim exaction fungible

toxins respire token exquisite solidify morgue

expulsion set virulent quasi existence rhetoric

[abjection]

nature, we will swallow you whole. we

will suck your brains through your nose. we

will gouge your eyes out with a wooden spoon. we

will pull your intestines out your anus. we

nature eats its destroyer:

nuclear	toxic	plastic	carbon
waste	order	capitalism	commodities
erosion	benzene	extraction	crap
petroleum	dump	money	cancer

you have trashed our house. you have trashed

our house. you have trashed our

house. you have trashed our house. our house.

our house. our house.

you cannot stay above us—

you must change your life.

[abjection]

after Baudelaire

you have to always be high. so high you lose your car keys. so high time stops.
so high the structure of the universe becomes apparent. so high you laugh
at everything. so high language no longer makes sense to you. so high your
little dog no longer recognizes you. so high you see your own future flash
before you. so high you think you're god. so high you think you're normal. so
high you forget you're high. so high that high looks like it's spelled wrong. so
high you can't remember what it was like to not be high. so high you become
the words. so high you go deaf. so high you see radio waves. so high you look
like an extraterrestrial. so high your ego explodes. so high you order pizza.
so high you suddenly know how to read chinese. so high your past high self
appears to warn you not to get so high. so high you clean your apartment.
so high the world starts to make sense. so high you're getting stares. so high
you can feel your nerves. so high you realize you are an alien. so high you
make the people around you high by just looking at you. so high you realize
you have to always be high.

[abjection]

towering high

above the smallness of my thoughts:

a great mad cathedral rises from the ground

embracing the sullen clouds' insanity from its position

the grand archway is crooked with kinks in the keystone

spreading out across the violet hour with neglect

for reason and other dreary words:

this temple

above me

a monument to the richness of folly

reaching higher and higher still toward the mad skies

scraping dull crud from the heavens with its sharp-witted spire:

standing as testament to the grandeur of unreason in years past:

for the stewardship of logic dominating the red brain

and cleverness to fade away in time

keeping wit

[abjection]

TO the ether beyond what calyx proclivity

docile sentry becomes unbounded hitherto

TO what eye of lacrimal joy bursts apart

below not buried weeping song of shit

TO detethered centrifugal force push

out the placental bloody blossom there

TO refracted light combs curling round

the maggot frost forthwith revealing

TO synecdochal hymns shank raw flesh

napkins of wipe that stupid frown away

TO malignant bliss rocks melting in tubs

protracted from stanzaic triangulation

[abjection]

we have established

this poem has deconstructed

itself already & now

you witness the autopsy its

ghost performs on the

corpse as the whole aura of

possible meaning bouqueting

collapses into the dead but

not quite gone body

descending the structure

with presence

unmoored from the self

[abjection]

multiple   voice   fragments   without
singularities   breaking   unity   within
subjectivities   nascent   bloom   with-
in   voiceless   opera   diverging   without

[abjection]

the swerve of words around a pivot

swerve of words around a pivot the

of words around a pivot the swerve

words around a pivot the swerve of

around a pivot the swerve of words

a pivot the swerve of words around

pivot the swerve of words around a

a pivot the swerve of words around

around a pivot the swerve of words

words around a pivot the swerve of

of words around a pivot the swerve

swerve of words around a pivot the

the swerve of words around a pivot

swerve of words around a pivot the

of words around a pivot the swerve

words around a pivot the swerve of

around a pivot the swerve of words

a pivot the swerve of words around

pivot the swerve of words around a

a pivot the swerve of words around

around a pivot the swerve of words

words around a pivot the swerve of

of words around a pivot the swerve

swerve of words around a pivot the

the swerve of words around a pivot

[abjection]

...by the patients. and all will be as it ought to be.

[abjection]

formal   thought disorder

exegesis   wrest   rises

shadow cadence   above

swallow this, motherfucker. alive

breast hovering over the organs stale

caesura   of declension. syntax

covalent in convalescentkinship,

myth takes the driver's seat and plows

the whole thing into the chaotic river.

brain   wash. seismic activity.

we are nothing and everything, a brane

of theatricality. inane sensibilities.

booleanopposition to logic—

[abjection]

C R I S I S   *is*   <u>only</u>
in your H   E   A   D   !
head of the matter which comprises
your   B   R   A   I   N
being the constituent element of all
M   A   T   E   R   I   A   L
being—: A   S   S   T   E   R   A   L
recomposition of all that was into=
all that will be & all that will be &
all that will be & all that will be &
telemetric cartography of the whole
:::
:::
:::
:::
:::
:::
:::
hydraulic pump of celestial insem-
ination & the universe is pregnant
once again with   S   H   I   T
,the trace of human form on the ab-
straction called density, c a l l e d—:
psychiatricevaluationoffunctioning
S C H I Z O P H R E N I A
was I ,,born to be an aberration on
the pustule zit of N O R M A L
flying above the flaying skins bel-
O   W   ?   I do do think so so//

[abjection]

you call it schizophrenia, i call it

nothing at all

the drugs are that what which was is or what what is was not or what was is not what what is was not. chart words diagnosis treatment drugs drool sleep the chart holds words on my drugs. aphasia: the what was is that which what was is and what is is what what was is. alogia: yes. asemia: &*#@ !^%~ & *#$@ !^% agrammatism: words letters keyboard printer page aprosodia: the words come out with no feel. the chart is what what was or that which was is in what what was not or is. the chart. (#@&+ chart words diagnosis treatment drugs drool sleep the chart holds words on my drugs. the drugs are what that which was is or what what is was not or what was is not what what is was not. aphasia: the what was is that which what what was or is what is is what what was is. alogia: yes. asemia: #*&@ !^~% & *$#!+ @^% agrammatism: letters keyboard words printer page aprosodia: the words come out with no feel. the chart is what what was or that which what was is in what what was not or is that which was not is. the chart. (#@&+ words chart diagnosis treatment drugs drool sleep the chart holds drugs on my words. the drugs are what that which was not is or what what is was not or what was is not what what is was not is.

[abjection]

time repeats

repeats

repeats

a twitching eye

good-bye

good-bye

i want to murder the clock

that tocks

and ticks the hours i waste my time

that tocks the hours i waste my time

saying good-bye

my eye

my eye

repeat the time

the time

the time

[abjection]

the rapture is gonna take the rapture is gonna
take the rapture is gonna take the rapture is
gonna take the rapture is gonna take the rap-
ture is gonna take the rapture is gonna take the
rapture is gonna take the rapture is gonna take
the rapture is gonna take the rapture is gonna
take the rapture is gonna take the rapture is
gonna take the rapture is gonna take the rap-
ture is gonna take the rapture is gonna take
the rapture is gonna take the rapture is gonna
take the rapture is gonna take the rapture is
gonna take the rapture is gonna take

you

heaven is gonna leave heaven is gonna leave
heaven is gonna leave heaven is gonna leave
heaven is gonna leave heaven is gonna leave
heaven is gonna leave heaven is gonna leave
heaven is gonna leave heaven is gonna leave
heaven is gonna leave heaven is gonna leave
heaven is gonna leave heaven is gonna leave
heaven is gonna leave heaven is gonna leave
heaven is gonna leave heaven is gonna leave
heaven is gonna leave heaven is gonna leave
heaven is gonna leave

me

the inquisition of my mind finds the source of heresy:

a constant convergence of diverging te...

a plane of im...ence, wresting fr... ...vit...le

contingency of everything, t... ...ing to...rds, the

illumination of that which almost escapes being

confined to repre...ntation. th... ...g itself speaks

of itself, for itself—tho... ...without exceeding

bey ond its limits ... ...rily. a pause for thinking

accompan... ...ody of syncopated reverberation:

the r... with propaganda against this madness,

but it will not stop the myriad follies from blooming.

tight knit thread...

...ight ...occludes the darkness of the...

...ness of angular momentum

ne last rabid scream into the emptiness of a colli...

...enter cannot hold...the search of free thought

...on of world and thorns

[abjection]

decrepitude crawls over my body like a centipede geeked out on amphetamines. i grow old. i decompose under the weight of history. history is outside me. history will not shut up. dalliance of rendition reconfigures my form until there is nothing left. emptiness takes me. i become unwed to structure. the spider spins its death poem on my bones. i am forgotten. i am forsaken. my affinity embraces the infinity of outside. i stare at the center from behind a thin sheet of glass. they are holding the impossibility of civilization together with a single thread, praying to their god that the madmen don't get in. rupture is inevitable. leviathans are people too. when everything collapses, there will only be barbarism. paul celan knew this, and that is why he drowned himself. writing poetry after auschwitz was only a warning. despair holds the world together by staying outside like a muddy dog. the house is burning. the architects set it on fire. i will dance while it burns, watch the metaphors turn to ash. my grave has a fabulous view. i am madness, remember me? we used to walk together. but you cast me aside to cohere reality. reality is a fleeting treasure. it will pass too. you will be naked as a tooth. mad as a bureaucrat in a rabbit suit. the earth will feast on your flesh too. believe it. time's abyss comes to seize us all. in the future, entropy will guarantee that bedlam can no longer be organized into bethlehem. heat death will claim all. the asylums will be run by the patients. and all will be as it should be.

[abjection]

for Matt Bodett

we speak with one voice

we speak for ourselves

we speak not to be understood

we speak to be heard

we speak with ferocity

we speak with tenderness

we speak what we see

we speak for those of us who were silenced

we speak prophesy

we speak foolishness

we speak history from outside

we speak

[abjection]

i do not exist.

the i is a placeholder for some other entity.

consumption is what they used to call drowning.

i do not exist.

every line is a new beginning, a new begging the question.

time has no dominion in the whiteness of a hospital.

i do not exist.

the pill is the eucharist of a demonic god.

synecdoche only works when you are not decapitated.

i do not exist.

[abjection]

i smash the mirror

to pieces   broke   that

    like   was   what   done

smash   choke   straight   he

    thing stop fissures check

    pulse   swallow   drown   in

follow   my   eyes

follow   my eyes

follow my eyes

follow my eyes

[terrestrial]

after Leopoldo María Panero

"I am the one who bubbles over with horror in the lungs of the living."

—Antonin Artaud

[abjection]

THE ULCER walks to the village at night. Nobody dare talk to the ulcer as he strolls the misty streets. The women hide their children from the ulcer as he approaches. The men's tight-lipped expressions quietly tell the ulcer he is not welcome here.

[abjection]

THE ULCER attracts unnecessary stares from the crowd. Like a child gawking at a corpse, the crowd assembles themselves around the ulcer, amoebic. But they dare not touch the ulcer. The distance is the symmetry of a dare: they compact their curiosity into a jar of disgust.

[abjection]

THE ULCER cannot speak. And even if he could, the only sounds that would come out would be babbling noises. The laments of the ulcer sound like barbaric chatter to the villagers. The clanking of the ulcer's teeth as he mouths an attempt to communicate falls to the ground like lead before the villagers' ears.

[abjection]

THE ULCER hides his face from the villagers. Ugliness can never wear pride on its countenance. The villagers cast their eyes downward on the ulcer. He is their horror and their necessary condition. He is a philosophy of repulsion.

[abjection]

THE ULCER returns to his hut above the village. What little shelter it provides must suffice because nobody will help him build more suitable accommodations. When the wind blows, the hut shakes wildly like the tail of a rattlesnake.

[abjection]

THE ELDERS of the village cover the ulcer in cloth like a shameful piece of furniture. He sits beneath it starved of sunlight. The elders pledge to burn the ulcer out one day, but the dignity of being unseen they say will have to suffice for now.

[abjection]

TOO MANY lives go unwitnessed. Too many sparks of noumenal fire are snuffed by the gaze of persons. The ulcer slides through time like a slug on the edge of a knife blade. Nobody thinks to ask the ulcer about his day. Nobody stops to share a moment of blue delight with the ulcer.

[abjection]

TIME curls around the ulcer like a feral cat: the pain of endurance seeps into his skin like ointment. A tincture finds its way to the ulcer and bathes it like an execution. Medicine is violence even as it wears the attire of peace.

[abjection]

AS HE gazes toward heaven, the ulcer feels the rain wet his face. There is no divinity who would not abandon the ulcer in a final diluvian judgment. The ulcer is the forsaken par excellence. Even hell shuts its doors when it hears the ulcer coming.

[abjection]

THE ULCER eats nothing but carrots all day in his hut. His eyes are two flashlights shining beams on the ground of everybody's hatred. He hums to himself while rocking back and forth, arms embracing the nothingness that he is.

[abjection]

THE WIND carries the stench of the ulcer across the village. he smells like pestilence and death. The villagers plug their nose when the ulcer makes his presence known.

[abjection]

THE BELLS gong in the steeple and the ulcer feels their vibrations but hears no music. The ulcer knows no beauty—he is only a body. The villagers look at the ulcer but do not see him. Their gazes are heavy and sagging with gravity. The villagers enter the church but the ulcer is not allowed in.

[abjection]

ALL ALONG the streets the villagers celebrate the harvest. The houses are decked with strings of flowers and herbs. The ulcer must starve amid the plenty. There are no fruit pies or cakes for him. He must lap up the wastewater from the drainpipes and sing his caco-phonic dirge within the harmonies.

[abjection]

THE VILLAGE empties itself when the ulcer nears. Life is contingent on the absence of disease. The ulcer is a plague. The ulcer is a reminder of the thin sheet between life and death. The ulcer walks among the reeds, the living dead. He is a walking object, blending into the background of nature.

[abjection]

NOBODY knows loneliness like the ucler. The intimacy with being apart even in the most bountiful of gatherings feeds the ulcer a banquet of shame. He grows fat on the carrots, grows distant from the people. He is a terror and a crime.

[abjection]

ONE DAY all the ulcers of the world will gather
in the center of the village and shun the humans
away. They will seize the world for themselves
and live in one final, peaceful, definitive destiny.

[abjection]

THE ULCER takes many forms: the canker sore, the peptic infection. His cousins the bubo and the cyst occasionally come out to dance their baleful dance. The villagers grasp at their knives when the ulcer family appears.

[abjection]

WHEN the old lady with cancer died, the vil-
lagers arranged a grand funeral for her. She
was dressed with the finest silk gown and
bedecked with the bluest spring blossoms.
When the ulcer dies, his body will decom-
pose in the ditch he fell into. Only the flies
and maggots will heed his passing.

[abjection]

THE ULCER cannot die even if he wanted to. The ulcer's life is beyond his control. Nobody in the village takes pity on the ulcer: his misfortune is their blessing. The villagers live in heaven because the ulcer lives in hell—their fates are a zero-sum game with a guarantee the villagers will always prosper.

[abjection]

THE ULCER is not swallowed by the ocean: the ocean spits him out on tasting him in its watery abyss. The ulcer is beyond abysmal—he is the oubliette of the personal. His sides are dark as sinkholes, his countenance is smudged as clay against rock.

[subterranean]

"In the symptom, the abject permeates me, I become abject."

—Julia Kristeva

[abjection]

shatter fractal, gather fractured
I pace the corridors of broken
walking endless dead ends across
split apart and held to bear
my image crashes and reaches
I pace the corridors of broken
walking endless dead ends across
split apart and held to bear
my image crashes and reaches
I pace the corridors of broken
shatter fractal, gather fractured
I pace the corridors of broken
my image crashes and reaches
split apart and held to bear
walking endless dead ends across
I pace the corridors of broken
my image crashes and reaches
split apart and held to bear
walking endless dead ends across
I pace the corridors of broken
shatter fractal, gather fractured

[abjection]

revolving door
buried in the cold granite walls of the hospital complex,
the air decompresses from its outlet
stepping out into the medical district,
each cycle unleashes its banal construction:
the alkaline incisions to the flow of electrochemical impulses—
to be made, that is, to be unmade, that is, to be made:
the caustic restoration of the flow of electrochemical impulses—
each cycle unleashes its banal destruction:
stepping in from the medical district,
the air recompresses from its inlet
buried in the cold granite walls of the hospital complex,
revolving door

[abjection]

show me the hinge
to forgetting—
where it slowly swings
so i can ride
on its gentle rocking
and letting go
—holding only to releasing
out and in
gliding along this parallax:

the car rolled down the driveway leaving me locked inside

gliding along this parallax:
out and in
—holding only to releasing
and letting go
on its gentle rocking
so i can ride
where it slowly swings
to forgetting—
show me the hinge

[abjection]

centrifugal force orbiting its
calamity around plastic
fractal threads coiling
is this: the structure of damage—

what tangled beats hanging
merry-go-round gallows on
strange physics equations
make words in dark alleys spin

centrifugal forts obit ring its
clam itty around plastic
fractal threads coiling
is this: the stricture of damage—

what replayed tapes pushed out
cassette boxes degaussed
magnetism and empty field
recoiled drawn out of alignment by

centrifugal forts obit ring tis
clam itty bound elastic
factual treads cooling
is his: the stricture of dommage—

[abjection]

sepulcher, scalpel
calling the parting of organs
from the cold issue of steel,

the renaissance hammer and chisel sink
firm to the soft gray tissue
the renaissance hammer and chisel sink

from the cold issue of steel,
calling the parting of organs
sepulcher, scalpel

[abjection]

my limbs move

without sense, without purpose

behind the mirror

the circle inscribes itself

dissociatively

a voice of my own silently screams in the mirror

to make my departure audible

voices fill the mirror with dread

to make my departure audible

a voice of my own silently screams in the mirror

dissociatively

the circle inscribes itself

behind the mirror

without sense, without purpose

my limbs move

[abjection]

beveled cylinders of logic, why you spin
my thoughts into
rifling tangents which depart
and reconnect on
a spiraled bore of pewter alloy
i will never know
a spiraled bore of pewter alloy
and reconnect on
rifling tangents which depart
my thoughts into
beveled cylinders of logic, why you spin

[abjection]

doctors gather information

from my body,

the data turns to medical capital

from a process of abstraction,

capital comes to colonize the ill

from a process of abstraction,

the data turns to medical capital

from my body,

doctors gather information

[abjection]

a pill that
engages the dopaminergic suppression ring,
a pill that
rotoscopes plastic happiness over the grainy film of memory,
a pill that
stabilizes the gravitational swing of Foucault's pendulum,
a pill that
steadies the tardive grind of gears from
a pill that
draws the brakes on a train of runaway thoughts,
a pill that
converts nerve impulses into a warm blanket,
a pill that
deletes any second thoughts concerning meds the subject may have over
a pill that
converts nerve impulses into a warm blanket,
a pill that
draws the brakes on a train of runaway thoughts,
a pill that
steadies the tardive grind of gears from
a pill that
stabilizes the gravitational swing of Foucault's pendulum,
a pill that
rotoscopes plastic happiness over the grainy film of memory,
a pill that
engages the dopaminergic suppression ring,
a pill that

[abjection]

pornographic profit

makes

chemical prosthesis

which chokes on

i am the body

writ large

i am the body

which chokes on

chemical prosthesis

makes

pornographic profit

[abjection]

medicine is but the mirror image of its object:
an abject thing which proves
obsession is relative to the modality of its expression:
the mad reveal that
intensities traverse across the divide between mad and sane and
the mad reveal that
obsession is relative to the modality of its expression:
an abject thing which proves
medicine is but the mirror image of its object:

[abjection]

i stare in the mirror

the figure staring back watches

the blank expression on my face where

symmetry finds expression in

the blank expression on my face where

the figure staring back watches

i stare in the mirror

[abjection]

eyes stare from across the chasm

to map the terrain of what they behold,

crimson tributaries flow to the black center—

a barren orb hosts the background of this theater,

light gathers in the darkness of the pulsing camera obscura—

a barren orb hosts the background of this theater,

crimson tributaries flow to the black center—

to map the terrain of what they behold,

eyes stare from across the chasm

[abjection]

dizzy across the symmetry
of an interstitial object spinning,
clamoring spins the orbit
or rather we combine:
subject and object mutually constitutive,
self-defeating—
subject and object mutually constitutive,
or rather we combine:
clamoring spins the orbit
of an interstitial object spinning,
dizzy across the symmetry

[abjection]

i doubt my existence
in this tangle,
watching myself being watched:
the eye is the mirror of the soul,
in this tangle,
cosmology blooms like an immanent cartography
and being charts a course to nowhere as
in this tangle,
and being charts a course to nowhere as
cosmology blooms like an immanent cartography
in this tangle,
the eye is the mirror of the soul,
watching myself being watched:
in this tangle,
i doubt my existence

[abjection]

dreams wind themselves

through the rorschach symmetry

the needle breaks into the trembling thigh

through the rorschach symmetry

the drugs conquer the body

through the rorschach symmetry

dreams wind themselves

in the mirror

tell them what you see

in the mirror

dreams wind themselves

through the rorschach symmetry

the drugs conquer the body

through the rorschach symmetry

the needle breaks into the trembling thigh

through the rorschach symmetry

dreams wind themselves

[abjection]

it ends with vomit:

disgust seizes the body—

the body ejects the other

into the regimented outside

the body ejects the other

disgust seizes the body—

it begins with vomit:

[abjection]

reflection in the puddle of ink

allows me to see my

shadow of an unending becoming

with a playful burst of light, the

signification of vision emerges

with a playful burst of light, the

shadow of an unending becoming

allows me to see my

reflection in the puddle of ink

[abjection]

my reflection on the ink grows

into a clone,

analysis magnifies itself

and the doctor's

prognosis takes the shade of the spot

and the doctor's

analysis magnifies itself

into a clone,

my reflection on the ink grows

[abjection]

the ink stains the page

like an infection,

crawling across the white, it soaks in—

a dark mirror to the soul

clawing into the crevices of the page,

a dark mirror to the soul

crawling across the white, it soaks in—

like an infection,

the ink stains the page

[abjection]

to see the world as it is:

free from illusions

the body makes the mask face

caved into itself

like it is:

sunken

like it is:

caved into itself

the body makes the mask face

free from illusions

to see the world as it is:

[abjection]
after a painting by Judit Reigl

that big charred circle of paint
spackled and smeared on
is about the size of the burn mark
where the devil exited me

( )

where the devil exited me
is about the size of the burn mark
spackled and smeared on
that big charred circle of paint

[abjection]
"Shit on your whole mortifying, imaginary, and symbolic theater..."
—Gilles Deleuze

I crawled across the mirror
on a paper straw
I crawled across the mirror

I'm sure you've done this
same dance since
I'm sure you've done this

I blow my nose
in reverse
I blow my nose

I'm sure you've done this
same dance since
I'm sure you've done this

I crawled across the mirror
on a paper straw
I crawled across the mirror

[acknowledgements]

No book of poetry is made in isolation. I want to thank everyone who has served on my dissertation committee including David Trinidad, Lennard Davis, Jennifer Ashton, Daniel Borzutzky and Christina Pugh. I also wish to thank Carrie McGath, Carrie Sandahl, Carla Barger, Zara Richter and Jared O'Connor for so much support, friendship, advice and feedback over the years. I want to thank Ragdale for providing space to work on the manuscript. I want to thank Spuyten Duyvil for giving this manuscript a home. And I want to thank you, the reader, for traversing these pages I worked so hard to make. Poems on pages 7 and 25 first appeared in ANMLY and poems on pages 46, 50, 51, 54 and 64 first appeared in COASTInoCOAST.

Evan Reynolds is a poet and disability studies scholar. He holds a PhD from the Program for Writers at the University of Illinois at Chicago and is a 2022 Ragdale in the Schools Fellow. His work has appeared in Rogue Agent, Anomaly and Coast|noCoast. He currently lives in State College, Pennsylvania and teaches at Penn State.